EVERYWHERE IS JERUSALEM: LEADER GUIDE

Everywhere Is Jerusalem:
Experiencing the Holy *Then* and *Now*

Everywhere Is Jerusalem
978-1-7910-3132-9
978-1-7910-3134-3 eBook

Everywhere Is Jerusalem: Leader Guide
978-1-7910-3133-6
978-1-7910-3135-0 eBook

Everywhere Is Jerusalem: DVD
978-1-7910-3136-7

James C. Howell

EVERYWHERE IS JERUSALEM

Experiencing the Holy *Then* and *Now*

Abingdon Press | Nashville

Everywhere Is Jerusalem
Experiencing the Holy Then and Now
Leader Guide

978-1-7910-3133-6

MANUFACTURED IN THE UNITED STATES OF AMERICA

CONTENTS

CONTENTS

To the Leader

Welcome to the leader guide for *Everywhere Is Jerusalem*! Whether your group consists of young adults, retirees, young parents, singles, or some combination of all of these, you are sure to find plenty of content for engaging all participants. *Everywhere Is Jerusalem* is part travel memoir, part spiritual autobiography, and part devotion, offering readers a rich look at how the spiritual geographies of our world fit onto the contours of our hearts and our relationships with God. From Rome to Jerusalem, from Selma to cemeteries, James Howell teaches us that God can be found everywhere, and that considering holy sites opens the door for us to consider more closely how our own spiritual walk intersects with the paths that saints have trod.

In this leader guide, you'll find included the resources you need to lead your group with confidence (and hopefully as little stress as possible). Each of the six sessions includes guidance on preparing for the session (including both materials needed and practices for getting ready), opening activities and prayers, discussion and reflection questions, and closing activities and prayers. You are free to use as much or as little of the leader guide content as you need. As is often stressed throughout the leader guide, you know your group best. You know what activities will lead to meaningful spiritual experiences, and which will just be corny. You know what questions will generate discussion and what will lead to blank stares and long silences. Use your discretion in choosing activities, and feel free to get creative as well!

TIPS FOR LEADING A GROUP SESSION

- You may wish to set a conversation covenant before you begin. What do participants expect out of conversations? Respectful engagement? Confidentiality? Mindfulness about self-monitoring how much one is talking?
- Give time after offering a question for people to stop and reflect. Some people will not immediately have an answer, but if allowed to think, will come up with creative responses! Get comfortable with a little bit of silence.
- Use hands-on, creative activities to get the session flowing! Even adults need a little bit of kinetic fun.
- The more confident you are through having prepared, the easier the session will feel to lead.
- Monitor who in the group is talking and who is not. Feel free to address questions to individuals (if you don't think doing so will embarrass them), or use a talking stick or stone to regulate participation.
- Mix it up! Consider using conversation pairs if big group conversation is going slowly.
- Honor the time. Start and end on time (except by agreement of the group).

USING TECHNOLOGY TO LEAD

- Most activities given in the leader guide are adaptable to a digital platform. Consider in advance what you'll need to tell participants to have ready (for example, writing implements, a bowl of water, colored pencils, and so on).
- Practice using the platform you're going to implement! Get a friend or family member to log in to the meeting with you to help you explore all the features of the platform.
- Send participants digital reminders and links to the meeting in advance.
- Encourage participants to use the "mute" feature to minimize background noise.
- Make use of features such as chat rooms to give participants a chance to talk in pairs or small groups.

SESSION 1

Everywhere Is Galilee

The Downward Call

PLANNING THE SESSION

Learning Objectives

By the end of this session, participants will:

- Become familiar with *Everywhere Is Jerusalem;*
- Define pilgrimage and what it means in Christian Scripture and culture; and
- Begin to understand their own lives through the lens of pilgrimage.

Materials

- Index cards (one for each participant)
- Writing implements for each participant
- Time-keeping device

- Copies of book
- DVD

Getting Ready to Lead

- Read chapter 1, "Everywhere Is Galilee: The Downward Call," closely.
- Watch session 1 on the *Everywhere Is Jerusalem* DVD.
- You know your group best! Jot down whatever questions come to mind that you think might generate good discussion.
- Gather suggested materials.
- Decide on a structure for your meeting that works best for you! You might begin with the suggested opening activity, have the bulk of the time spent on discussion, and close in prayer.
- Read through the selected questions in this guide. Select a few to focus on, with others as back-up as time allows.
- Spend some time in solitude and prayer as you prepare to lead a meaningful group.

OPENING ACTIVITY AND PRAYER

Opening Activity

Distribute an index card and writing implement to each participant. Ask each participant to write on the card:

- One place that is sacred to them. It doesn't have to be a church or a traditional holy site. Possible examples: a family member's house, a spot in nature, the setting of a cherished memory, somewhere where they experienced God's presence in a special way.
- Why is this place important to them?

Use a timer, bell, or other time-keeping device. Give everyone 2-3 minutes to write and reflect. Then, have everyone pair up with a partner. Each person has 1 minute to share. Call everyone back to the large group. Invite anyone to share what their sacred place was.

Opening Prayer

Journeying God,
We thank you that we,
Wayfaring strangers,
Meet each other here.
As we study from story, Scripture, and place,
Let us find you close by.
Amen.

WATCH DVD SEGMENT

Play session 1: "Everywhere Is Galilee" on the *Everywhere Is Jerusalem* DVD or via Amplify Media.
Discuss:

- Did anything specific stand out as you watched the video?
- What is something you learned that you didn't know before?

Invite the group to keep both the video and the book in mind throughout the discussion below.

STUDY AND DISCUSSION

"The Jesus Boat"

- The author discusses what it must have been like for the disciples, some of them fishermen, to answer Jesus's

call to follow him. What do you imagine it must have
been like for them to receive this call? What did they
give up to follow Jesus?

- Have you ever followed Jesus on a journey you weren't
expecting? What was that like for you?

"Down, Down, Down," "Sitting Around in Paris," and "The Dexter Avenue Parsonage"

- James Howell describes his call story. Keeping in mind
that God calls all of us to different places, careers, and
relationships (not just pastoral ministry), do you have
a "call story"? How would you describe it?
- St. Francis embraced risks and family rejection from
following God's call. Has discipleship ever been costly
for you? How so?
- James Howell describes several more contemporary
individuals (Mother Maria, Dorothy Counts, and
Martin Luther King Jr.) who modeled faithful response
to God's call. What other "saints" would you name as
inspiring your own path?
- When we confront injustice in our own times, how can
looking to figures like these help?

"St. Francis of Lithuania"

- James Howell discusses how God's call can meet us
in unexpected places—for him, Lithuania. Where are
unexpected places in which you have met God?

"Not Jesus's Girlfriend"

Mary Magdalene has often, falsely, been identified as a prostitute
(or even as Jesus's girlfriend). While neither of these things make her

less worthy of God's love, they have limited how we have historically understood her discipleship. James Howell discusses how, sometimes, personal factors of our identity determine how others see us and can sometimes try to restrict how we live out our calling.

- Have you ever experienced this?
- How do you remain faithful to your calling even when you run into these barriers?

"What Kind of a Christian Are You?"

- How would you answer the question posed to the author during his travels: "What kind of a Christian are you?" What is most important to share about your faith?
- If people look at your life, what do you think they would find out about God? In other words, what kind of gospel is your life preaching?

"Living with Moses"

The author reflects, "How can I stick closer to the kind of Christian God asks me to be? Could I commit to a sustained lifetime of reading, pondering, reflecting, praying, conversing, going down, far from the place of comfort?"

- Consider your own response to these questions. What do you hope your path of discipleship looks like going forward?

"My Aching Knees"

- The author writes, "Do I seek just comfort from God? Does God want me to be as comfortable as possible?" How would you answer these questions?

- What points from the chapter will stick with you the most as you move forward this week? Are there any topics that haven't been discussed that you'd like to share with the group?

CLOSING ACTIVITY AND PRAYER

Closing Activity

Invite the group into a few minutes of quiet reflection. With writing materials and the index card from earlier in the session, invite participants to write a few words or draw a picture to illustrate what shape their pilgrimage takes today. They might draw a symbol that evokes the idea of pilgrimage to them. Invite participants to share in pairs and/or in the broader group.

Closing prayer

Holy God,
You have called us to be a pilgrim people.
Go with us, we pray,
Though the road may be long,
And our destination uncertain.
No matter where our lives have taken us,
You have always guided us back home to you.
Reassure us in that knowledge.
In the name of the refugee Prince of Peace,
Amen.

Everywhere Is the Jordan

Baptism and All the Waters

PLANNING THE SESSION

Learning Objectives

By the end of this lesson, participants will:

- Reflect on the theological significance of water;
- Trace the role of water in biblical stories from Old Testament to New Testament; and
- Consider what role remembering their baptism may have in their spiritual pilgrimage moving forward, enacted through ritual.

Materials

- Index cards for each participant
- Writing implements for each participant

- Time-keeping device
- Copies of book
- Basin
- Water

Getting Ready to Lead

- Read chapter 2, "Everywhere Is the Jordan: Baptism and All the Waters," closely.
- Watch session 2 on the *Everywhere Is Jerusalem* DVD.
- You know your group best! Jot down whatever questions come to mind that you think might generate good discussion.
- Gather suggested materials.
- Decide on a structure for your meeting that works best for you. You might begin with the suggested opening activity, have the bulk of the time spent on discussion, and close in prayer.
- Read through the selected questions in this guide. Select a few to focus on, with others as back-up as time allows.
- Spend some time in solitude and prayer as you prepare to lead a meaningful group.

OPENING ACTIVITY AND PRAYER

Opening Activity

Give participants one minute to jot down every song they can think of that has to do with water. Compare lists with a partner for 1 minute more. Then see how many *different* songs the group has recalled!

Opening Prayer

Holy God, you encounter us
   In the dripping of rain water;
   In the depth of the ocean;
   In the splash of a pond,
   In the holy waters of baptism.
You call us, claim us, and know us.
Greet us here today again,
      And empower us to feel your presence today.
Amen.

WATCH DVD SEGMENT

Play session 2: "Everywhere Is the Jordan" on the *Everywhere Is Jerusalem* DVD or via Amplify Media.

Discuss:

- Did anything specific stand out as you watched the video?
- What is something you learned that you didn't know before?

Invite the group to keep both the video and the book in mind throughout the discussion below.

STUDY AND DISCUSSION

"And A River Runs Through It"

James Howell writes, "The whole spectacle of water, so much of it, flowing forever but so very fresh, so now, and the mind-boggling cause of the massive mountains and valleys that stand so solidly as mute witnesses to the power of what you can't cup in your own hand: so humbling, inspiring so much awe, maybe even faith in God."

- What does water symbolize to you?

The author reflects, "I'm happy never to have attempted to preach in such a place, as the trio of mountains over my shoulder would steal all the attention, a more eloquent witness to God's grandeur than any sermon could muster."

- What experiences of God have you had in nature?

"Remember Your Baptism"

- The author associates the waters of baptism with the water of birth. How do you understand the connection between baptism and birth?

Baptism, James Howell explains, has to do with identity. He writes, "Baptism announces to the world who you really are, and who all the others are as well..."

- Who do you think baptism tells the world "[we] really are, and who all the others are as well"?
- Does baptism give us a new identity, or does baptism unveil an identity we already have?
- Are there any stories about your own baptism you would like to share?

"The Wonder of Baptismal Fonts"

- Howell reflects on a few different baptismal fonts that he has encountered in his travels. What kind of baptismal font is used in your worship space? Is there a special symbolism or history to it?
- How do you respond to the author's story about the baptismal font in Belmont Abbey that used to be a slave trading block? What are the moral complexities of this re-usage?

"As a Hart Longs for Flowing Streams"

The author writes, "It's not just thirst. There is clearly pain. 'My tears have been my food / day and night, / while people say to me continually, / "Where is your God?"' [Psalm 42:3]. We cannot guess at the psalmist's trouble. You can fill in the blank with your own. The water we need, the water we are, the waters we shed in sorrow."

- What is your "water" in times of sorrow? What sustains you?
- What are some of the examples that Howell names of water showing up in stories of Jesus? What does Jesus's association with water suggest about what Jesus means to us?
- Howell writes, "He's the one we're thirsty for." What thirsts does Jesus satisfy for us? Do any feel of more or less significance to you in your life today?

"Healing Waters"

The story of Naaman is one that we may be less familiar with than others that Howell talks about. Take some time to read 2 Kings 5, especially the part where Naaman experiences God's healing:

So [Naaman] went down and immersed himself seven times in the Jordan, according to the word of the man of God; his flesh was restored like the flesh of a young boy, and he was clean.

Then he returned to the man of God, he and all his company; he came and stood before him and said, "Now I know that there is no God in all the earth except in Israel; please accept a present from your servant."

(2 Kings 5:14-15)

- Why do you think water is such a powerful symbol of healing throughout the Bible? Can you relate to Naaman's reluctance to do the simple thing that would bring him healing? What is behind his reluctance, do you think?

"Geysers, Pools, and Other Dangerous Waters"

- Sometimes, Howell reminds us, water can be dangerous, and we need to heed the warning signs. How do we discern the difference between healing waters and dangerous waters in our spiritual life? How do we pay attention to the signs?

Sometimes water has been put to "unholy uses." He uses the example of how beautiful Yellowstone Park was created as a result of financiers' greed and displacing American Indians, to whom the land rightfully belonged.

- What are unholy uses of water that you have seen? Are there ways of purifying water once it has been polluted by injustice?

"Water Is Thicker than Blood"

- Howell describes some ways in which Christianity reverses the common adage, "Blood is thicker than water." How does baptism bind us together?

Sometimes our spiritual journeys can involve prioritizing ties of discipleship over ties of biological family. Howell describes how St. Francis and St. Clare fit this pattern. However, for many of us, family is very important.

- How do we hold in tension family commitments with the call of discipleship? What guidance does Jesus's calling of the disciples give us on this subject, and how does this intersect with our personal experiences?

"The Holy Family"

Howell writes, "The Bible portrays almost all the families in its long, sprawling narrative as highly dysfunctional. Could Jesus—if he truly came to be one of us, one with us—have had a squeaky clean, entirely peaceful, healthy family? Didn't they have their moments?"

- What do you think about Powell's question here? What do you think Jesus's family was like? What clues does the Bible give us, and what do you imagine?
- What does the Bible's depiction of "messy" families have to teach us about relating with our own families?

Howell writes, "The grace of God, the reality of God's church, doesn't bless our existing family so much as it creates a new sacred family."

- What does this statement mean to you? Have you experienced being part of a "sacred family"? What are its characteristics, in your experience?
- How can your church community become the most faithful "sacred family" it can be?

"Everywhere Is Water"

- Howell makes the connection that water, representing the sacred, is already in and around us, before we even do anything. How does this knowledge shape our spirituality?

- How can we tap into the experience of the presence of God being all around us and within us in our day-to-day living?

CLOSING ACTIVITY AND PRAYER

Closing activity

Set a basin of water in the midst of the group. Invite each member, as they feel led, to dip a hand in the water and remember their own baptism. Invite each member of the group to say a single word about what baptism means to them.

Closing prayer

God of the Jordan,
    God of all waters,
We remember your promises,
    So often communicated through water.
As we depart today, make us intimately aware of your presence,
    Flowing through us.
Let our awareness of that presence strengthen our sense of sacred worth,
    And the sacred worth of all who pass through the waters
    with us.
Amen.

SESSION 3

Everywhere Is the Mount of Olives

Standing Up and Courage

PLANNING THE SESSION

Learning Objectives

By the end of this session, participants will:

- Consider what courage as a spiritual quality means to them;
- Relate this definition of courage to stories of Scripture; and
- Commit to future communal and/or individual action that embodies courage on behalf of the vulnerable.

Materials

- Index cards for each participant
- Writing implements for each participant

- Time-keeping device
- Copies of book

Getting Ready to Lead

- Read chapter 3, "Everywhere Is the Mount of Olives: Standing Up and Courage."
- Watch session 3 on the *Everywhere Is Jerusalem* DVD.
- You know your group best! Jot down whatever questions come to mind that you think might generate good discussion.
- Gather suggested materials.
- Decide on a structure for your meeting that works best for you. You might begin with the suggested opening activity, have the bulk of the time spent on discussion, and close in prayer.
- Read through the selected questions in this guide. Select a few to focus on, with others as back-up as time allows.
- Spend some time in solitude and prayer as you prepare to lead a meaningful group.

OPENING ACTIVITY AND PRAYER

Opening Activity

Ask everyone to write down a definition of what constitutes courage, setting a timer for 2 minutes. Then pair participants for 2 minutes to discuss and compare their answers. Coming back to the large group, ask participants to share anything from their pairs that feels particularly important.

Opening Prayer

God of the martyrs, God of the cross,
You know all our fears.

You see every injustice.
You call us into courage,
Even when our voices shake and our knees tremble.
Fill us with your strength and boldness,
  To act on your will,
    And to stand up for justice for the marginalized.
Amen.

WATCH DVD SEGMENT

Play session 3: "Everywhere Is the Mount of Olives: Standing Up and Courage."

Discuss:

- Did anything specific stand out as you watched the video?
- What is something you learned that you didn't know before?

Invite the group to keep both the video and the book in mind throughout the discussion below.

STUDY AND DISCUSSION

"Jesus's Immense Courage"

- Is courage a characteristic that you have often associated with Jesus? Why or why not?

James Howell writes, "He was calling the Romans out, along with those religious authorities who knuckled under to the lie that faith shouldn't confront the government but just get along."

- This statement suggests that Jesus's ministry was, at least in part, political. How does the idea that Jesus's ministry was political sit with you? Does it challenge you, anger you, or comfort you?

Going on, Howell writes, "He [Jesus] was taking sides with the destitute and despised, the nobodies and the disenfranchised."

- How does this statement feel to you? Do you believe that God takes sides? Why or why not?
- Does God ask us to take sides too? What about when positions the church might take are controversial and might drive some people with different ideas away?

The author writes, "Holy Week didn't surprise Jesus. He had decided in advance to make his stand. When? During his ministry? in the desert? at his Baptism? as a boy?"

- Have you ever thought about these questions before? Do you think Jesus knew what was coming for him? Was his confrontation with authority something that he had planned in advance, did it arise naturally from how he loved others in the world, or some other possibility?

"Here I Stand. God Help Me."

- James Howell recounts how these words are a quote of Martin Luther, put on trial for his unorthodox (at the time) religious beliefs and stances regarding Church doctrine. Why do you think the last three words of this quote ("God help me") were so important to Luther?
- Have you had a "Here I stand" moment? How was standing up for what you believed in right for you? What helped you to be courageous at that time?

"One of Us Should Stand with Her"

Howell writes, "The mandate isn't to be a Christian in the privacy of our souls, or in church with people like us. Just as God chose to stand with us in our humanity, we keep an eye out for moments when we can stand *with*. Our journey? Get off the couch, out of the house and the church, and we go and stand."

- Here, Howell emphasizes standing *with*. How is standing *with* someone different from speaking up for someone? What is the goal of standing with someone?

"Good Trouble Crossing a Bridge"

- The late congressman John Lewis is famous for describing his civil rights work as "good trouble." What does the phrase "good trouble" mean to you?

Howell writes, "There's something in the journey of faith about crossing bridges, building bridges, and even being a bridge. The Latin word for "priest," *pontifex*, means bridge-builder. That's what a priest, a pastor—and even a regular lay Christian—does: she or he is a bridge between people and God, between the challenges of the world and the life of God."

- Being a "bridge-builder" may be an unusual way of thinking about Christian identity. What would it mean to you to be a "bridge-builder"? Can being a bridge-builder also involve confronting systems of power?
- Jesus, Howell argues, was himself a bridge-builder. However, Jesus himself said that he did "not come to bring peace but a sword" (Matthew 10:34). How do you reconcile these two ideas?

"St. Francis, Courageous Peacemaker"

- Why does it take courage to make peace? Have you experienced stories of courageous peacemaking in your own life?
- Where in our world do we need courageous peacemakers to step into situations of conflict?

"As for Me and My House"

- Where do you see courage showing up in the stories of God's people in the Bible? How do you differentiate courage from violence?

Howell writes, "Wherever you stand or sit, right now, you have to make a decision, and a hard, serious one. It's not some vague spirituality or sliding into a pew now and then. Choose your God or your gods! Take a stand; make this journey—and live it, with courage, grit, patience, maybe making that definitive decision again. And again."

- Where do you feel called to take a stand in your own life?

"Give Me That Bible Stuff"

Howell narrates the story of the founding of Koinonia Farm and its conflicts with the Ku Klux Klan due to its prophetic position against racism. For Clarence Jordan, the Bible was full of profound statements against racism. However, for others throughout the history of North American chattel slavery, the Bible was used to promote oppression.

- How do you make sense of this?
- Are there times you can be "excused from being a Christian for fifteen minutes"? Why or why not? How about when our families and children are threatened?

"Unrevealed Until Its Season"

- Howell discussed Luther's labors in translating the Bible into German. How do you think the rarity of having access to Scripture in your native language would affect you? How are things different now?
- Sometimes songs spur courage. Howell gives the example of how "A Mighty Fortress Is Our God." Are there any songs that have given you particular courage?

"The Day the Phone Rang"

- How is courage sometimes going into hiding? How do characters in Scripture sometimes bide their time for the right moment to act?

The story of Dietrich Bonhoeffer may be familiar to some readers, but it can also deeply affect us. Bonhoeffer lived away from Nazi Germany for a time but returned to stand in solidarity with those who suffered under the Third Reich. He wrote,

> We have to learn that personal suffering is a more effective key, a more rewarding principle for exploring the world in thought and action than personal good fortune.

> We can have an abundant life, even though many wishes remain unfulfilled.

> Nothing that we despise in the other man is inherently absent from ourselves. We must learn to regard people less in the light of what they do or omit to do, and more in the light of what they suffer.

- Consider these quotes. Is there one that stands out to you? What do they mean to you?

- Suffering has traditionally been a major theme in Christian theology. More recently, some theologians have pushed back on this theme by pointing out that putting suffering on a pedestal can encourage people who are already abused and oppressed to suffer more or tolerate their mistreatment, quite unfairly. How do you respond to these ideas? How do you square them with the history of martyrdom in Christianity?

Howell quotes Marilynne Robinson, author of *Gilead* and other works. She writes,

> Theologians talk about a prevenient grace that precedes grace itself and allows us to accept it. I think there must also be a prevenient courage that allows us to be brave—that is, to acknowledge that there is more beauty than our eyes can bear, that precious things have been put into our hands and to do nothing to honor them is to do great harm.

- What would "prevenient courage" look like to you? How might you experience prevenient courage in your life?

"The Passion to Be One with Jesus"

Howell describes how St. Francis's passion to be one with Jesus led him to desire to experience even Jesus's suffering. Ultimately, this meant that he received stigmata, bleeding wounds that symbolized his oneness with Christ.

- How do you respond to this story? Does it feel foreign and unpalatable, or spiritually meaningful to you?
- What does oneness with Christ mean to you? Does it have a physical connotation? an emotional connotation?

31

- Where do you long for oneness with Christ in your life?

St. Francis crafted a prayer, which Howell quotes, to express his desire with oneness with Christ:

My Lord Jesus Christ, I pray You to grant me two graces before I die: the first is that during my life I may feel in my soul and in my body, as much as possible, that pain which You, dear Jesus, sustained in the hour of Your most bitter Passion. The second is that I may feel in my heart, as much as possible, that excessive love with which You, O Son of God, were inflamed in willingly enduring such suffering for us sinners.

- What would you say to God to express your desire for unity?

CLOSING ACTIVITY AND PRAYER

Closing Activity

Discuss where, in your community or society, the church may be called to courage. Where might God be asking you to say, as Jesus's actions during Holy Week proclaimed, "Here I am. Here I stand"?

Closing Prayer:

Holy God,
Even as we prepare to move apart from one another,
Let our desire for oneness with you keep drawing us together.
Though physical space may separate us,
Let our desire to courageously embody and proclaim all that you have taught,
Continue joining us in one heart, mind, and soul.
Amen.

SESSION 4

Everywhere Is Bethlehem

Prayer Walls

PLANNING THE SESSION

Learning Objectives

By the end of the session, participants will:

- Understand the spiritual value of lament as prayer;
- Reflect on walls that divide and walls that bring together our prayers; and
- Grow in faith that in times of trouble, God hears our cries.

Materials

- Sticky notes for each participant
- Writing implements for each participant
- Time-keeping device
- Copies of book

Getting Ready to Lead

- Read chapter 4, "Everywhere Is Bethlehem: Prayer Walls."
- Watch session 4 on the *Everywhere Is Jerusalem* DVD.
- You know your group best! Jot down whatever questions come to mind that you think might generate good discussion.
- Gather suggested materials.
- Decide on a structure for your meeting that works best for you. You might begin with the suggested opening activity, have the bulk of the time spent on discussion, and close in prayer.
- Read through the selected questions in this guide. Select a few to focus on, with others as back-up as time allows.
- Spend some time in solitude and prayer as you prepare to lead a meaningful group.

OPENING ACTIVITY AND PRAYER

Opening Activity

Create a "prayer wall." Using sticky notes (or the "chat" feature if in Zoom meeting virtually), list areas of pain in your life, in the lives of loved ones, or in the world. Spend some time in reflection about the laments you would like to raise to God. Then place them on the wall alongside the laments of others in the group.

Opening Prayer

God of sorrows,
Hold us in this space.
Hold our grief.
Hold our pain.

Hold this aching world.
Help us to see each other,
   And know each other,
   And love each other,
     In this space.
Amen.

WATCH DVD SEGMENT

Play session 4: "Everywhere Is Bethlehem: Prayer Walls."
Discuss:

- Did anything specific stand out as you watched the video?
- What is something you learned that you didn't know before?

Invite the group to keep both the video and the book in mind throughout the discussion below.

STUDY AND DISCUSSION

"Wailing Walls"

James Howell briefly quotes Ephesians 2:14, which is part of a larger passage from Ephesians. As a group, read the following passage. You might even read it multiple times, in the manner of Lectio Divina, taking time to reflect on a single word or phrase.

So then, remember that at one time you gentiles by birth, called "the uncircumcision" by those who are called "the circumcision"—a circumcision made in the flesh by human hands—remember that you were at that time without Christ, being aliens from the commonwealth of Israel and strangers to the covenants of promise, having no hope and without God in the world. But now in Christ Jesus you who once were far off have been brought near by the blood of Christ. For he is our peace; in his flesh he has made both into one and has broken down the dividing wall, that is, the hostility between us, abolishing the law with its commandments and ordinances, that he might create in himself one new humanity in place of the two, thus making peace, and might reconcile both to God in one body through the cross, thus putting to death that hostility through it. So he came and proclaimed peace to you who were far off and peace to those who were near, for through him both of us have access in one Spirit to the Father. So then, you are no longer strangers and aliens, but you are fellow citizens with the saints and also members of the household of God, built upon the foundation of the apostles and prophets, with Christ Jesus himself as the cornerstone; in him the whole structure is joined together and grows into a holy temple in the Lord, in whom you also are built together spiritually into a dwelling place for God.

Ephesians 2:11-22

- What does this passage teach you about Jesus's mission, particularly having to do with walls? How do walls help us? How do walls separate us?
- What experiences of walls do you have? How does this chapter's discussion challenge or enrich your understanding of this passage?

"Jesus in Montgomery and Gethsemane"

- How does the idea of a "wailing God" affect you? What questions does it bring to your mind, or what questions does it help you address?
- Howell reflects, concerning Jesus's agony in the garden, "Could he have said *No*?" Is this a question you have considered before? What thoughts do you have about it?

- Would a Jesus who could say no mean something theologically different than a Jesus who can only say yes to his suffering?

"The Patron Saint of Worried Mothers"

Consider the short poem "Don't Worry" by Mary Oliver that is quoted in the book (page 75).

- Knowing St. Augustine's story, including his mother's agony, how might you respond to this poem? Is there comfort for the weeping mothers, from Monica to the woman Howell observed praying in the Italian church?
- How do we honor the grief and struggle of parents who worry about their children?

Howell writes the following about prayer: "Prayer isn't magic. But it does bind us tightly, like twins or like mother and child, to those for whom we pray, and to God. God knows our pains over children who struggle. After all, God watched his own beloved Son suffer such a terrible death on the cross. Prayer is love."

- What, to you, is the importance of prayer? If prayer doesn't necessarily mean that the child is safely delivered or all is well, what is its importance?

"The Patron Saint of the Pandemic"

Howell dubs Julian of Norwich "the patron saint of the pandemic" because she lived in isolation during the bubonic plague in Europe, and her spiritual insights during that time can be transformative for our own spirituality.

- Think back to your own time of pandemic isolation. How did the pandemic affect you emotionally? What did the pandemic make you think about? What spiritual revelations, if any, came from your experiences of pandemic isolation?

"The Cathedral Was for God"

Howell writes, "What is a church building if it's not a place, not just to pray, but to teach us how to pray, more expansively, and in communion with others?"

- How do you respond to Howell's question? What do you understand as the chief purposes of church architecture?
- How do we balance aesthetic beauty with practicality? Does the beauty of church spaces serve others, or is it more important to allocate resources toward more direct means of service?

Reflect on these questions of Howell's:

"Think about it: artists created these unnecessary works of art, knowing they couldn't be seen by worshippers or anybody once the building was finished. Hidden wonders—but not hidden from God. They were crafted only for God's eyes to behold. Like a holy life: it's for God."

- How do such marvels inform our prayers in the more average sanctuaries and homes where we find ourselves?
- What benefits, if any, does worshipping in architecturally lovely places have for our communal and/or personal spiritualities?

"Praying for the Queen"

Howell describes how going to church with his children changed his perception of what was important to experience in church. He writes, "I wish I could say my little children were enthralled with the idea of returning for—prayer? and to hear a small choir sing sacred music? But we came. Lots of fidgeting and yawns…"

- How has worshipping with children shaped your experience of worship? Have you learned anything from children's spirituality?

Howell writes, "Praying isn't just praying your needs. Prayer is getting caught up into the needs of God's world. If you pray in your house, you're unlikely to pray beyond your own needs. But in an unfamiliar church or out in God's world? We'll discover Karl Barth was right: 'To clasp the hands in prayer is the beginning of an uprising against the disorder of the world.'"

- Have you ever found that going to a different place has changed what you have prayed for? How so?

"The Labyrinthine Way to Jerusalem"

- Have you ever prayed using a labyrinth? What was that experience like for you?
- Sometimes prayers are not merely words, but also embodied. Are there any prayer practices that you follow that are especially embodied? How does using your body to pray change the experience of prayer for you, if at all?

Howell writes, "How moving is it that when we trace our steps along a labyrinth, we are united with Christians both now and in the Middle Ages in Chartres—and so many other places around the world!"

- What other experiences of Christian practices have given you the feeling of being connected other Christians around the world?

"Teeming with Life"

Howell informs his readers, "Medieval cathedrals were designed to represent the glories of God's creation indoors."

- What worship spaces, if any, have given you the sense that you are close to the glory of God's creation?

Howell writes, "Worship is a time and space apart from the world in order for us to find our way out into the world. Worship isn't a man-made place distinct from the beauty of the natural world; at its best, church is a place where we realize God's glory in the world we find ourselves in."

- What do you think Howell means by this? How does worship help us encounter God's glory in the world?

"A Mighty Fortress"

Howell tells the story of how St. Francis, along with other medieval people, thought that an earthquake accompanying Jesus's crucifixion caused every cleft and fissure in rocks, even as far as Italy.

- What new meanings does this story give to phrases like, "Rock of Ages, cleft for me"?
- In times of trouble, like the Roman siege, ancient peoples sometimes fled to high, rocky places like Masada. What kind of faith would it take to sustain a

community during times like those? Is this a faith that church communities of which you are part have?

"Of the World, but Not Worldly"

- Howell makes the point that one sacred place can remind you of another. What experiences have you had in which experiences in one holy site recalls another one?
- Howell uses the phrase "willing withdrawal" to describe moments of spiritual pilgrimage. What does this phrase mean to you? What does "withdrawal" mean within the life of faith? How do we balance withdrawal with activism?

"The Our Father"

- For many people, the Lord's Prayer is ingrained as a meaningful recitation fundamental to their faith life. What does the Lord's Prayer mean to you? How has it shaped your faith?
- How does beginning the Lord's prayer with the address to God as "Father" affect you, positively or negatively? What, to you, does it signal about how Jesus asks us to approach God?

Howell ends this chapter with a challenge to us: "'Lord, teach us to pray.' We echo the ask of the disciples. Can you make some sort of wall and write on it, or in it? Do you have a kitchen table? Any interesting trees nearby? Who's wailing nearby or in the world? And whom else might you forget in your prayers? What is hidden that God sees? And what's right out in the open that is holy, but you'd missed it?"

- How will you respond to the challenge? How could your prayer life deepen and respond more fully to the needs of the world and the needs of your own heart?

CLOSING ACTIVITY AND PRAYER

Closing Activity

Revisit the prayer wall made in the opening activity. Invite participants to select a sticky note from the wall, written by another participant, to take home with them, possibly to begin their own prayer wall practice. They might consider placing the sticky note on a bathroom mirror or a place they'll view regularly.

Before departing, invite participants to voice their own prayers of lament. Candles could be lit as a reminder of the light of Christ in the midst of the troubles of the world.

Closing Prayer

Lamb of God,
You hold the pain of the world,
And yet you hear the cries of our individual hearts as well.
In your death,
You show God's radical openness to all who suffer,
Hanging on the cross in solidarity with the world.
Bring us peace, Holy One.
When the night is dark,
Be the star that ushers us home.
In the name of Christ,
Amen.

SESSION 5

Everywhere Is Nazareth

Finding the Way Home

LEARNING OBJECTIVES

By the end of this lesson, participants will:

- Understand "home" as a theological concept;
- Connect with their own, and others', emotions about home; and
- Grow in faith that God is our home even when we wander.

PREPARATION

Materials

- Writing implements for each participant
- Time-keeping device

- Copies of book
- Whiteboard: physical or virtual

Getting Ready to Lead

- Read chapter 5, "Everywhere Is Nazareth: Finding the Way Home."
- Watch session 5 on the *Everywhere Is Jerusalem* DVD.
- You know your group best! Jot down whatever questions come to mind that you think might generate good discussion.
- Gather suggested materials.
- Decide on a structure for your meeting that works best for you. You might begin with the suggested opening activity, have the bulk of the time spent on discussion, and close in prayer.
- Read through the selected questions in this guide. Select a few to focus on, with others as back-up as time allows.
- Spend some time in solitude and prayer as you prepare to lead a meaningful group.

OPENING ACTIVITY AND PRAYER

Opening Activity

Brainstorm about the idea of "home" through the five senses for 2 minutes: Sight, hearing, smell, taste, and touch. What does the idea of "home" evoke for you? Can you think of what home looks, sounds, smells, tastes, and feels like to you? Is there a specific place that comes to mind?

Time the group for 2 minutes, listing as many ideas or connotations as you can on the whiteboard. Spend a couple of minutes reviewing and discussing your list, then move to the opening prayer.

Opening Prayer

God who calls the prodigal, call.

Call out to us once more today.

Let us walk in to your loving arms.

Let us know your powerful, welcoming hospitality for us,

   No matter where our journeys have led us,

   No matter how far from home we have wandered.

We are wanted.

We are loved.

We are home with you.

Amen.

WATCH DVD SEGMENT

Play session 5: "Everywhere Is Nazareth: Finding the Way Home."
Discuss:

- Did anything specific stand out as you watched the video?
- What is something you learned that you didn't know before?

Invite the group to keep both the video and the book in mind throughout the discussion below.

STUDY AND DISCUSSION

"At Home in Nazareth"

- Have you ever thought about what Jesus was like as a child, or what his home life was like for him? What do you imagine?

Howell mentions Luke 4:16-30 as a reminder that homegoing is not always easy, even and especially not for Jesus! Read this passage and consider:

When he came to Nazareth, where he had been brought up, he went to the synagogue on the Sabbath day, as was his custom. He stood up to read, and the scroll of the prophet Isaiah was given to him. He unrolled the scroll and found the place where it was written:

"The Spirit of the Lord is upon me,
because he has anointed me
to bring good news to the poor.
He has sent me to proclaim release to the captives
and recovery of sight to the blind,
to set free those who are oppressed,
to proclaim the year of the Lord's favour."

And he rolled up the scroll, gave it back to the attendant, and sat down. The eyes of all in the synagogue were fixed on him. Then he began to say to them, "Today this scripture has been fulfilled in your hearing." All spoke well of him and were amazed at the gracious words that came from his mouth. They said, "Is not this Joseph's son?" He said to them, "Doubtless you will quote to me this proverb, 'Doctor, cure yourself!' And you will say, 'Do here also in your hometown the things that we have heard you did at Capernaum.'" And he said, "Truly I tell you, no prophet is accepted in his hometown. But the truth is, there were many widows in Israel in the time of Elijah, when the heaven was shut up for three years and six months and there was a severe famine over all the land, yet Elijah was sent to none of them except to a widow at Zarephath in Sidon. There were also many with a skin disease in Israel in the time of the prophet Elisha, and none of them was cleansed except Naaman the Syrian." When they heard this, all in the synagogue were filled with rage. They got up, drove him out of the town, and led him to the brow of the hill on which their town was built, so that they might hurl him off the cliff. But he passed through the midst of them and went on his way.

- What do you think is so troubling or offensive to the Nazareth people, that they try to kill Jesus? Why is rejection their first reaction?
- St. Francis had a similar experience to that of Jesus, of being rejected by some of those who knew him best. Why do you think that religious leaders such as Jesus and Francis have this experience?

Howell writes, "God seems to have fashioned us with this hankering for home, and yet with gnawing sensation that you're never quite there. You might own and dwell in a fancy house. But 'home' is...well, who can say?"

- Does your own experience match with this statement? Why or why not?
- Howell quotes a few songs that revolve around the theme of "home." Can you think of favorite songs or sayings that have to do with home? What significance do these songs or sayings have to you?
- Often, the journeys God calls us on lead us away from home. Just think of Abraham leaving Ur! Why does God call us away from home, while also giving us a desire for home?

"My Childhood Home"

- What special places stand out to you about your childhood home? What makes these places memorable to you?

- Howell recounts how he has had desires to revisit childhood homes, even telling a story of how he got to go inside one such home. This was true for him in spite of the difficult childhood experiences he had there. Does Howell's experience seem relatable for you? Why or why not?

Howell writes, "'Home' is such a prevalent and powerful biblical and theological theme. The good gift of a home, not necessarily the house, yet often in a house, is itself a great grace, stirring an awareness of belonging and safety, even in homes that are less than ideal. Maybe this is the deep reason we pray for and work for those who are homeless, or immigrating, or coping with disaster."

- How does lack of a stable place to rest our heads affect us, physically, emotionally, and spiritually? Where does our Christian commitment to care for the homeless and displaced come from?

"A Second Home"

- Howell shares a story about a "home" that was different from where his family lived. What types of places gave you a sense of love and belonging that were not "homes" in the strictest sense?

Howell writes, "Could it be that the function of a place away from home, a second home, with beloved grandparents, infusing so much grace and shimmering with love and belonging, might be to help us know how to think about a longed-for home, 'not made with hands, but eternal in the heavens,' so we might believe, and yearn, and even be patient in the waiting? Do we believe in a better place because we've spent time in...a better place?"

- How do you respond to this quote? Why do you think God gives us a longing for home, especially when that longing cannot, immediately, be satisfied?

"Where Did the Lord's Supper Happen?"

- What does "the Lord's Supper" mean to you? Is it possible to experience it somewhere that is not, strictly speaking, a church Communion table or altar? Why or why not?
- How do meals give us a sense of home? Why are meals so useful for building community?

Howell explains that the site in Jerusalem traditionally attributed to Jesus's Last Supper with the disciples may not be where the meal took place, but he says, "Yet I am not flummoxed in the least that we cannot pinpoint where Jesus shared that Last Supper with his disciples. I'm even appreciative. Why? Wherever it happened in the year 30 CE, I am moved by the mystical miracle that this very meal also happens on Sunday mornings in my sanctuary, in prisons and nursing homes, and has happened in churches where I've worshipped and even preached in Scotland, Lithuania, Kenya, China, Brazil, and all over America—too many to number. Everywhere is that Upper Room."

- How does Jesus's last meal with his disciples transcend time and space?
- Howell then restates his point, "We are there, and then, with Jesus and the others. Jesus breaks the bread and shares the cup with them, with us." What does it feel like to experience this shift over time and space to be with Jesus?

49

- Howell states, "All the Bible's images of heaven envision it as a lavish feast where nobody eats alone." Why is this significant? How can churches respond to this reality?

"Nothing Can Separate Us"

Crucial to this section is Romans 8:31-39, which Howell quotes a selection of here:

> If God is for us, who is against us? ... Who will bring any charge against God's elect? ... Who will separate us from the love of Christ? Will affliction or distress or persecution or famine or nakedness or peril or sword? As it is written,
>
> > "For your sake we are being killed all the day long; we are regarded as sheep to be slaughtered."
>
> No, in all these things we are more than victorious through him who loved us. For I am sure that neither death, nor life, nor angels, nor rulers, nor things present, nor things to come, nor powers, nor height, nor depth, nor anything else in all creation will be able to separate us from the love of God in Christ Jesus our Lord.
>
> (Romans 8:31-39)

How does the knowledge that nothing can "separate us from the love of God" shape the way we respond to hardships, like those that Howell describes learning about in his trip to China?

- Nationalist pride often becomes intertwined with religion, as Howell learned in his pilgrimage to China. Indeed, nationality is one of the things that can give us a sense of "home." How, to you, are nationalism and faith related, if at all? What is the relationship between your Christian faith and a sense of national identity?

"Put Away the Gods Your Fathers Served"

Howell writes how his grandparents "were white Southerners during Jim Crow. It's foolish to judge people of prior eras by modern progressive standards. And yet, to reckon with what's in the soil of 'home,' and what's in our spiritual DNA may be a big piece of the puzzle in our own quest to find our way home to our true selves, and to God."

- How do we reckon with parts of our spiritual histories, sometimes delivered through our families, that are difficult, painful, or mismatched with what we consider Christian values today?
- What value lies in revisiting the racism or other forms of prejudice that form part of our stories?
- Howell quotes the narrative of the Israelites entering the Promised Land, in which they are exhorted to "put away the gods [their] fathers served." What "gods" may you be called to put away?

Howell writes, "What is the thoughtful Christian, yearning to be holy, to do? Avoid Fort Pulaski or St. Peter's in Rome? Or do we explain away the ugliness? Back then, people didn't know better, right? I wonder if the hard realities of such places—and they are everywhere!—are mirror images of you and me, beautiful, made in God's image, temples of the Holy Spirit, and yet so very broken, sinful, confused, even addicted to what is not of God and not healthy for our spiritual selves. And aren't such places the kind of places such beautiful and broken people are bound to produce?"

- What are your reflections on Howell's questions here?
- Howell presents Jesus as the ultimate example of learning to live with ambiguity. What kinds of

ambiguity does Jesus represent and experience? How does he live with the in-between, and how can we?

"Finding the Other Descendants"

- Lots of people have gotten interested in genealogy, as Howell describes. Is this a pursuit you have ever indulged? Why or why not?
- Howell describes his spouse's efforts to find the descendants of people her ancestors enslaved. Why do you think this is a meaningful quest for her?

"Wherever I Am"

Howell writes that, since our ultimate home is with God, we may struggle to feel fully "at home" anywhere we go. "But in the meantime, aren't there hints and manifestations of that ultimate home?"

- What are some manifestations of this ultimate home that you can experience today?
- How does the image of our home with God being like a mobile home, or an RV, strike you? Is this a useful way to depict our migratory relationship with God? Why or why not?
- Revisit these questions that are integral to the chapter. Think about them privately, then discuss as a group.
- "When you read the word *home*, what place comes to mind? Do you feel a warm coziness? Or do you tense up a little? Does no single place register in you? Do you have a sense of being at home where you live right now?"

CLOSING ACTIVITY AND PRAYER

Closing Activity

Draw the outline of a large house on a virtual or physical whiteboard, to represent the concept of "home." Invite participants to write in a word or short phrase about what home means to them.

Spend some time reviewing and discussing the image and words you have written, then move to the closing prayer.

Closing Prayer

God who is home,
Who draws us home,
We give you thanks for home.
For all these things about home named here:

[Participants should name words and phrases from the board.]

Let all homes be safe homes.
Let all homes be loving homes.
Let all people have a home.
Dwell in each home.
Amen.

*Before everyone departs, ask them to bring a favorite cross (or more than one, if desired) to share with the group next week. (See the opening activity in session 6).

SESSION 6

Everywhere Is Jerusalem

Places of Sorrow and Hope

PLANNING THE SESSION

Learning Objectives

By the end of this session, participants will:

- Begin to hold in tension the presence of life and death, sorrow and hope in Scripture and in their lives;
- Reflect on how memorializing the dead can draw us closer to God; and
- Consider how God is found in their own stories, even in difficult times.

*Prior to the session, invite all participants to bring a favorite cross (or more than one, as desired, to show and tell).

Materials

- Copies of book
- DVD
- Crosses brought by participants
- If desired: paper and drawing implements

Getting Ready to Lead

- Read chapter 6, "Everywhere Is Jerusalem: Places of Sorrow and Hope."
- Watch session 6 on the *Everywhere Is Jerusalem* DVD.
- You know your group best! Jot down whatever questions come to mind that you think might generate good discussion.
- Gather suggested materials.
- Decide on a structure for your meeting that works best for you. You might begin with the suggested opening activity, have the bulk of the time spent on discussion, and close in prayer.
- Read through the selected questions in this guide. Select a few to focus on, with others as back-up as time allows.
- Spend some time in solitude and prayer as you prepare to lead a meaningful group.

OPENING ACTIVITY AND PRAYER

Opening Activity

Give everyone a chance to share the crosses they brought from home. Notice different materials, words inscribed on the cross, size, shape, symbolism, and so on. Invite each person to share a brief story about where the cross came from and what it means to them.

Opening Prayer

> God of the cross,
> You unveil the hope in suffering,
> The life in death,
> And the joy in grief,
> All through the cross of Christ our Lord.
> Meet us here,
> Wherever we may find ourselves today,
> And let us see where you would have us carry our crosses.
> Amen.

WATCH DVD SEGMENT

Play session 6: "Everywhere Is Jerusalem: Places of Sorrow and Hope."

Discuss:

- Did anything specific stand out as you watched the video?
- What is something you learned that you didn't know before?

Invite the group to keep both the video and the book in mind throughout the discussion below.

STUDY AND DISCUSSION

"Maundy Thursday Late"

- Howell states that Maundy Thursday was when Jesus made the most significant decision about his fate. Do you agree, or do you see other moments of decision-making throughout Jesus's story?

Howell reminds himself that the soldiers arresting Jesus "fell to the ground" when they confront his identity, spoken with Jesus's simple words, "I am he." This, Howell points out, is simply what people throughout Scripture do when they meet God.

- What does it feel like to be faced with the divine? How do you react?

"Sacred Places of Sorrow"

- What does visiting cemeteries feel like for you? Do you seek cemeteries out, like Howell does? Do you avoid them? Why?
- What is the purpose of commemorating places of pain, such as the site of the Armenian genocide Howell describes, or Yad Vashem in Jerusalem? Are there any risks to this commemoration? If so, what? How does the presence of these memorials connect people to their past?
- A prominent phrase in contemporary justice movements has become, "Say their names." Saying names is also part of monuments to killed innocents. What is the significance of saying the names of victims? Is this a biblical concept? Why or why not?

Howell writes, "To draw close to the heart of God, we are to be attentive to death—honorable, courageous deaths; unjust, criminal deaths; natural deaths; and sudden deaths. And our spiritual journey is itself a journey toward death. We grow as we ponder the place where evil will be no more, where every tear will be wiped away. We ponder our mortality, the brevity of time that is ours, that this world isn't all there is."

- Why is attention to death important to God's heart? What, if anything, is the difference between what Howell is describing and being morbid?

"Not 'On a Hill Far Away'"

Howell describes the chaos at the site where the Crucifixion is commemorated today. It doesn't feel like a silent, serene pilgrimage site. But, Howell points out, this chaotic atmosphere might actually match what the Crucifixion scene was like.

- Why does this chaos help recall the scene when Jesus died?
- Howell makes the statement that crosses are "so easily trivialized." What do you think he means? How do you respond to this statement?

"Underground Portals to Heaven"

- Why do you think images of "life beyond suffering and death" were so significant and moving to early Christians, as in the catacombs of Priscilla? Do these kinds of images still have this kind of sway today? Why or why not?
- What stories of life overcoming death from the Bible are particularly important to you?

"You Never Stop Being Loved"

- Howell describes how he knelt at the graves of many people who were significant to him. Have you ever felt this type of reverence at someone's grave? What do you imagine caused him to kneel?
- Howell mentioned how, at these graves, he was led to pray in thanksgiving to God for their lives, and, in

some cases, to lament the circumstances that led to their deaths. When you think about people who, in their lives, inspired you, what do you feel led to pray to God about?

"Peter Is Here"

Howell discusses Peter's story of following Jesus, forsaking him, and ultimately being reconciled to him as emblematic of our Christian life. He writes, "Either way, we all stay in our graves, our columbariums, our urns, or even the depths of the sea, awaiting the hope Peter staked everything on, and quite courageously, travelling to Rome to preach and be arrested, imprisoned, tried, and probably executed."

- What inspiration do you find in Peter's story? Why might we look to Peter's grave for the hope that we, too, might fulfill our callings?

Howell quotes John 21:18: "When you were young, you girded yourself and went wherever you wished. But when you grow old, you will stretch out your hands, and someone else will carry you where you do not wish to go" (his translation).

- How does this verse strike you? Are there any points of resistance in you as you read it? If so, what are they?
- In response to this verse, Howell writes, "It's no longer what I want to do, or even what I want to do for God, but what God wants me to do." Does this statement reflect how you think of God? Why or why not?

"All Ye Citizens of Heaven"

Howell discusses how some surprising people are buried in churches. He ties these burials to David Ford's reflection that "'My

Father's house' might be unimaginably capacious, and even those most at home there might meet many surprises—especially other people they do not expect, but also dimensions of truth and life."

- What does Ford's quote mean to you? What might you encounter in "my Father's House" that you do not expect?
- How can we respond to the roominess of God's grace? What does it mean for you to live into this grace today?

"The Incorruptibles"

- The "resurrection of the body" has been a theme in Christian theology for millennia. Some, as Howell discusses, have taken this theme to an extreme in their efforts to commemorate departed saints. What does this theme of Christian faith mean to you?
- How does your belief in what happens to your body after you die shape your choices around end-of-life matters? How well does your church openly discuss these topics?

"Where Death Happens"

Howell writes, "Death happens in a hospital or out on a stretch of highway, and then the real death happens with family at home, and in the heart of God, and in the sacred places that are the church and loving memory. At the same time, our hope in the redemptive power of Jesus's death happens in all those places as well."

- What do you make of this statement? What is the "real death"? Where do you believe that the "real death" happens?

"Where I Didn't Want to Go"

- Howell's fifteen-day hospital stay was an unexpected confrontation with his mortality. What feelings does such an experience evoke? How do we learn to cope with the fact that we are mortal?

- Howell describes that he felt despair at times in the hospital. What brings us to despair in circumstances like a long hospital stay? What does Howell mean when he states that despair is "not something that mortifies Jesus"?

- Howell uses both "healing" and "curing" in his discussion. Do these two words have a similar or a different meaning to you? Can healing sometimes be found when a cure is absent? Why or why not?

- How can experiences like sickness reconnect us with what it means to be human, as Howell's hospital stay did for him?

- Howell ends his book with the story of his hospitalization. How might this hospitalization be another pilgrimage for him?

CLOSING ACTIVITY AND PRAYER

Closing Activity

Give everyone a few moments to reflect on this book study they've completed together. Then invite everyone to share one insight from the experience that they will take with them.

Discuss:

- How was the experience of studying this book about pilgrimage what you expected, or different from what

you expected? What will you take with you?
What will you leave behind?

If drawing implements are available, you might invite participants to draw an image from their experience.

Closing Prayer

God who holds our past, present, and future,
We offer all of ourselves to you,
Not understanding the mysteries of your life, death, and resurrection,
But trusting that you hold all things.
Send us into the world in peace,
Grateful emissaries of your love,
And as those who continue in our pilgrim way.
Amen.

Watch videos based on *Everywhere Is Jerusalem: Experiencing the Holy Then and* Now with James C. Howell through Amplify Media.

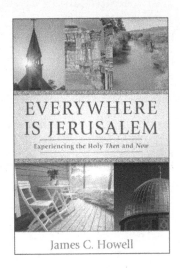

Amplify Media is a multimedia platform that delivers high-quality, searchable content with an emphasis on Wesleyan perspectives for churchwide, group, or individual use on any device at any time. In a world of sometimes overwhelming choices, Amplify gives church leaders and congregants media capabilities that are contemporary, relevant, effective, and, most important, affordable and sustainable.

With *Amplify Media* church leaders can:

- Provide a reliable source of Christian content through a Wesleyan lens for teaching, training, and inspiration in a customizable library
- Deliver their own preaching and worship content in a way the congregation knows and appreciates
- Build the church's capacity to innovate with engaging content and accessible technology
- Equip the congregation to better understand the Bible and its application
- Deepen discipleship beyond the church walls

Ask your group leader or pastor about Amplify Media and sign up today at www.AmplifyMedia.com.

Printed in the USA
CPSIA information can be obtained
at www.ICGtesting.com
LVHW030720070624
782371LV00006B/34

9 781791 031336